Death at an early age has a tendency to preserve, and oftentimes enhance, a star's fame, whether from film (Marilyn Monroe, James Dean) or music (Elvis Presley and John Lennon immediately becoming iconic figures this is the case with Martial arts superstar Bruce Lee. Due to his meteoric rise to fame in his short film career, we have been blessed with thousands of photographs of his life both on and off screen. Within these pages we capture his expressions as the camera clicked away firing of thirty six pictures in a roll of film. Enter the Dragon has more photos than any other movie he appeared in! Probably amounting to in excess of 10,000 images that were taken documenting almost every move he made. The one thing that stands out is the many emotions the camera captures from Bruce's facial expressions both in normal conversation and when he is in fight action mode. Within these collectors volumes we try to preservesome of these images by showing the sequences in which they were captured. Keeping the Movie legend alive that is Bruce Lee alive

"If you spend too much time thinking about a thing, you'll never get it done. Make at least one definite move daily toward your goal." – Bruce Lee

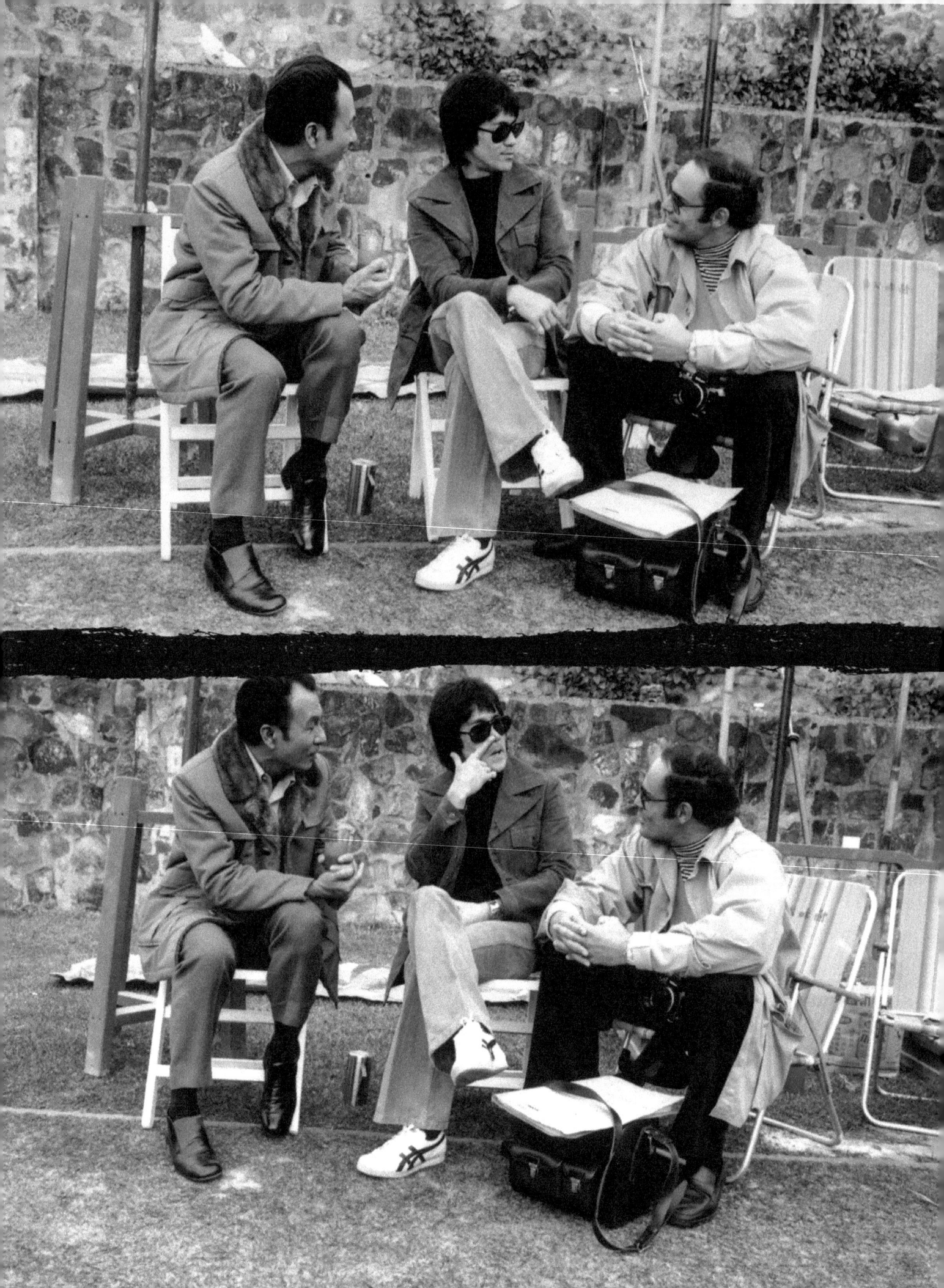

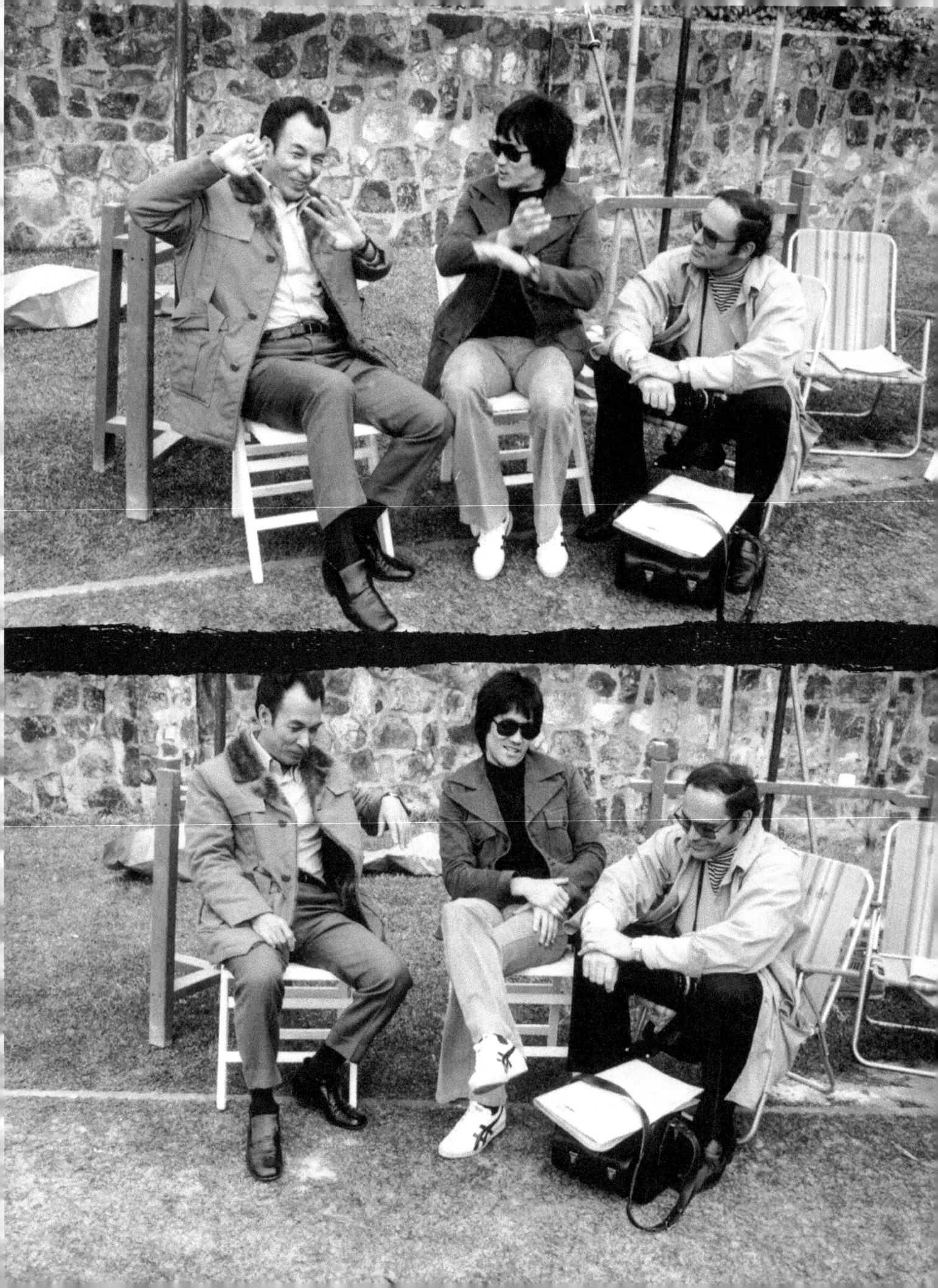

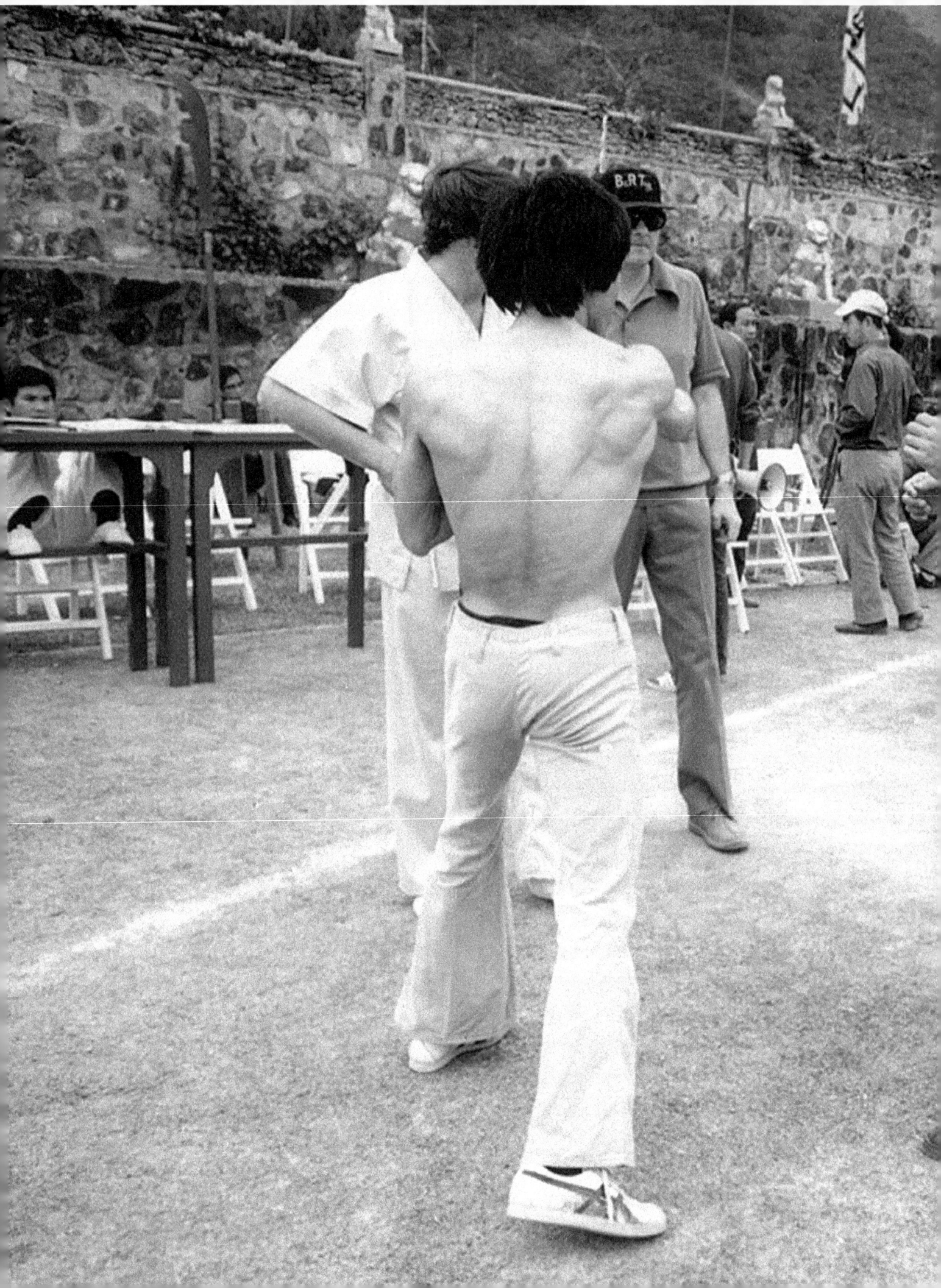

www.ingramcontent.com/pod-product-compliance
Lightning Source LLC
Chambersburg PA
CBHW051317110526
44590CB00031B/4388